I'm A Mommy

HUMMINGBIRD

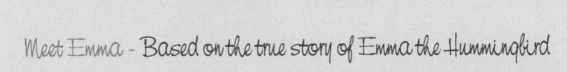

Meet Emma - Based on the true story of Emma the Hummingbird

STORY AND PHOTOS BY

Diane Davani

ISBN: 0615517595

ISBN-13: 9780615517599

Cover photo purchased from Dreamstime.

For Alex and Katie
I love you.

This book belongs to:

I'm a Mommy hummingbird,
Tiny, shiny and smart.
I take care of my babies,
With much love in my heart.

I zip and I zoom,
From one place to another.
But most important of all,
I'm an amazing mother.

I drink a drink called nectar,
It looks like water but it's sweet.
I can't just live on nectar though,
There are bugs I need to eat.

I catch spiders, flies and ants,
And once they're in my tummy,
I call it "buggy stew",
And I think it's really yummy!

When it's time to have my babies,
I make a perfect, tiny nest.
About the size of a walnut shell,
And I know how to make it best.

Actual Size

 6

I collect moss, and leaves, and spider webs,
And weave it all together.
It holds my growing babies,
Since it stretches and endures the weather.

I lay two little white eggs,
About the size of a pea.
Then I sit on them, to keep them warm,
Knowing they're safe under me.

And when they're ripe and ready,
About 17 days later,
They'll break their shell, and hatch.
There is no sight that's greater!

Larger Than Actual Size

When born they have no feathers,
And they cannot even see.
But in my eyes, they are beautiful,
And they love and need me.

Like little black wrinkled raisins,
With short triangle beaks,
They'll only stay in my nest,
About three short weeks.

When I fly to my babies,
Their beaks open wide.
I feed them "buggy stew",
And it fills them up inside.

They'll eat and they'll sleep.
And grow fluffy and tall.
Then when they're grown and ready,
The nest gets very small.

Then on one special day,
When all is right and good,
I tell my babies that it's okay,
To leave this neighborhood.

They fly from the nest,
And I join them where they land,
For I will help and teach them,
As God and nature has planned.

I help my babies learn,
About the sky, food and flying.
Then I tell them they must go.
I do so without crying.

My babies will have their own babies soon,
Starting families of their own.
But I will watch them, when I can,
Admiring the beauty I've sown.

Go forth, beautiful flying jewel babies,
And bless everyone you meet.

For the miracles you'll create for others
Is what makes life so sweet!

ABOUT THE AUTHOR

Diane Davani is a Southern California native who became intrigued (and consumed) with hummingbirds when Emma the Hummingbird began to build a nest in a wrought iron chandelier hanging from Diane's patio cover in her backyard. She had a hunch that others would enjoy seeing what she saw happening in Emma's nest, too. She was right.

Just 14 months after starting the live streaming of Emma's nest on the Internet, there were over 1.2 million views from 78 different countries. Emma became recognized worldwide in newspapers, television and most recently by Cornell University's NestCam program.

Diane is a licensed CA Real Estate Broker and enjoys cake decorating, exploring new places and things, and spending time with her husband and two great kids, Alex and Katie.

For more information about Diane and Emma the Hummingbird,
visit: www.OurHummingbirdNest.com

A MESSAGE FROM EMMA

ABOUT RED DYE IN NECTAR/FEEDERS:

Hummingbird feeders are designed with red parts to attract the notice of hummingbirds. Never add red food color to sugar water, and never use commercial mixes that have red dyes. Nectar in flowers is clear, and red food coloring has been shown in many studies to be harmful for hummingbirds. In taste test comparisons, hummingbirds have been known to choose the "homemade" version of sugar water anyway, so not only is it more economical to make your own, the hummingbirds like it better!

Here are easy directions for making safe hummingbird nectar:
1. Mix 1 part sugar with 4 parts water and bring to a boil to kill bacteria.
2. Let sugar water cool and fill feeder.
3. Extra sugar water may be stored in a refrigerator.

The two most important issues to consider in selecting hummingbird feeders are how easy they are to take apart and clean, and how large they are. Bacteria and mold grow in sugar water, and sugar ferments, so hummingbird water should never be left out for more than two or three days, and changed daily in very hot weather.

IN AN EMERGENCY

If you encounter a hummingbird who is in trouble, become disoriented, first, keep pets and kids away so they won't make the bird more anxious. If you have a hummingbird feeder with sugar water, offer the bird a drink by holding it close to the feeder, but don't try to force it. In cases where the hummingbird is not able to perch on the feeder, a syringe or dropper can be used to feed the hummingbird. Please be reminded that hummingbirds cannot live on nectar alone. This is only a temporary solution to stabilize the hummingbird.

HELP! I FOUND AN INJURED HUMMINGBIRD!

If you know your local hummingbird rehabilitation agency, call them immediately. For their phone number, look in the phone book or ask your local animal shelter, zoo, parks department, or conservation agent. Please also see these pages:

projectwildlife.org, iwrc-online.org or losangeleshummingbirdrescue.com

I FOUND A BABY HUMMINGBIRD. NOW WHAT?

The first thing you should do is nothing! Look around: is the bird's mother waiting for you to leave so she can feed it? (Only the mother participates in the nesting duties.) Occasionally, hummer nestlings fall over the side, but, like other birds, they're rarely abandoned by the parent. Then, see these pages: projectwildlife.org, iwrc-online.org or losangeleshummingbirdrescue.com. If you find a nest on the ground with eggs or chicks still in it, put it back. If unbroken eggs and live chicks are found out of the nest, put them back in. You may need to tie or tape a small box to the tree limb and put the nest inside (it doesn't have to be in exactly the same location, the mother will find her babies). Leave the top open. This is usually all you need to do; it's worked in many, many cases of nests knocked down in storms. Always wash your hands after handling any wild animal.

Your best course of action depends on the bird's state of development:

· **IF IT'S VERY YOUNG AND HELPLESS, NOT FULLY-FEATHERED:** If you can find the nest, put it back. If its mother doesn't appear in a half hour, call your local wildlife rescue organization. The mother may have been killed by a predator, window hit, etc., and the nestling will need rehabilitation help to survive. (Rehabbers are licensed only after extensive training, and it's not legal to capture or technically even touch a wild bird without state and Federal permits, except under the supervision of a licensed individual, so please don't expose yourself to legal problems. Caring for baby hummers is neither easy nor straightforward - e.g., most of their natural diet is partially-digested insects, shoved directly down their throats all the way into their stomachs. If you can't find a bird rehabber in the phone book, call your local animal shelter, zoo, parks department, or conservation agent to get the number.) If you can't return the bird to its nest, call wildlife rescue for instructions.

· **IF THE NESTLING IS WELL-FEATHERED AND CAN PERCH, BUT CAN'T FLY:** Put it back in the nest if you can. Otherwise, try to place it on an interior branch of a shrub, where it will be safe but its mother can feed it. Again, keep a lookout for the mother, and if she doesn't appear, or if the baby won't stay in the nest, call the rehabber. Feathered-but-flightless hummingbird nestlings often jump out of the nest if orphaned.

If it's not apparently anxious, it may simply be a fledgling in the process of learning to fly, and the best thing you can do is keep children and cats away until it flies off. If it's relentlessly calling for its absent mother, it may be an orphan in need of re-hab. If it's injured, call wildlife rescue immediately. If you can't save the bird and it dies, the biology department of your university will appreciate the opportunity to obtain it as a study specimen; we know relatively little about hummingbirds, and every opportunity to learn more helps the ones still alive and still to be born.

Please accept that not every baby bird will grow to adulthood; some are de-formed, some are sick, and some are just unlucky. No North American humming-bird is endangered, and natural selection favors individuals that survive without our help. This is how species become more successful, which must outweigh the welfare of any single bird. The decision to help is yours alone, and no one need feel guilty for action or inaction. But please call the pros for advice before risking making the situation worse; in many ways, young hummingbirds are not like our other familiar species, and few "civilians" are equipped to care for them properly.

One more thing: while you are admiring a young bird or a nest, there may be other eyes looking at you. Predators such as crows, jays, roadrunners, cats, and mice all eat baby hummers – and may wonder what you find so interesting, and will investigate after you're gone. Use binoculars to watch from a distance as much as possible.

Made in the USA
Middletown, DE
15 July 2020